THIS JOURNAL BELONGS TO

_____

For permission requests, please contact the publisher at:
Mango Publishing Group
2850 S Douglas Road, 4th Floor
Coral Gables, FL 33134 USA
info@mango.bz

For special orders, quantity sales, course adoptions and corporate sales, please email the publisher at sales@mango.bz. For trade and wholesale sales, please contact Ingram Publisher Services at:
 customer.service@ingramcontent.com or +1.800.509.4887.

Tree Lover's Blank Journal

ISBN: (print) 978-1-64250-949-6
BISAC category code: SEL045000, SELF-HELP / Journaling

yellow pear ◖ press

Printed in the USA
CPSIA information can be obtained
at www.ICGtesting.com
JSHW060042150824
68134JS00028B/2595